EARTH AND SPACE SCIENCE

EARTH SYSTEMS

By Christina Earley

A Stingray Book

SEAHORSE PUBLISHING

Teaching Tips for Caregivers and Teachers:

This Hi-Lo book features high-interest subject matter that will appeal to all readers in intermediate and middle school grades. It may be enjoyed by students reading at or above grade level as well as by those who are looking for age-appropriate themes matched with a less challenging reading level. Hi-Lo books are ideal for ELL readers, too.

Each book appeals to a striving reader's age and maturity level. Opportunities are provided for students to read words they already know while encountering a limited number of new, high-interest vocabulary words. With these supports in place, students will read more fluently while increasing reading comprehension. Use the following suggestions to help students grow as readers.

- Encourage the student to read independently at home.
- Encourage the student to practice reading aloud.
- Encourage activities that require reading.
- Establish a regular reading time.
- Have the student write questions about what they read.

Teaching Tips for Teachers:

Before Reading

- Ask, "What do I know about this topic?"
- Ask, "What do I want to learn about this topic?"

During Reading

- Ask, "What is the author trying to teach me?"
- Ask, "How is this like something I already know?"

After Reading

- Discuss how the text features (headings, index, etc.) help with understanding the topic.
- Ask, "What interesting or fun fact did you learn?"

TABLE OF CONTENTS

EARTH SYSTEMS

Planet Earth is made up of **systems**.

These systems provide **resources** to support life.

They are responsible for changes on Earth.

The five major systems are the geosphere, the hydrosphere, the cryosphere, the atmosphere, and the biosphere.

Each system **interacts** with the others.

FUN FACTS

Earth is about 4.54 billion years old.

WORD STUDY: The word part *sphere* means “ball-shaped area.”

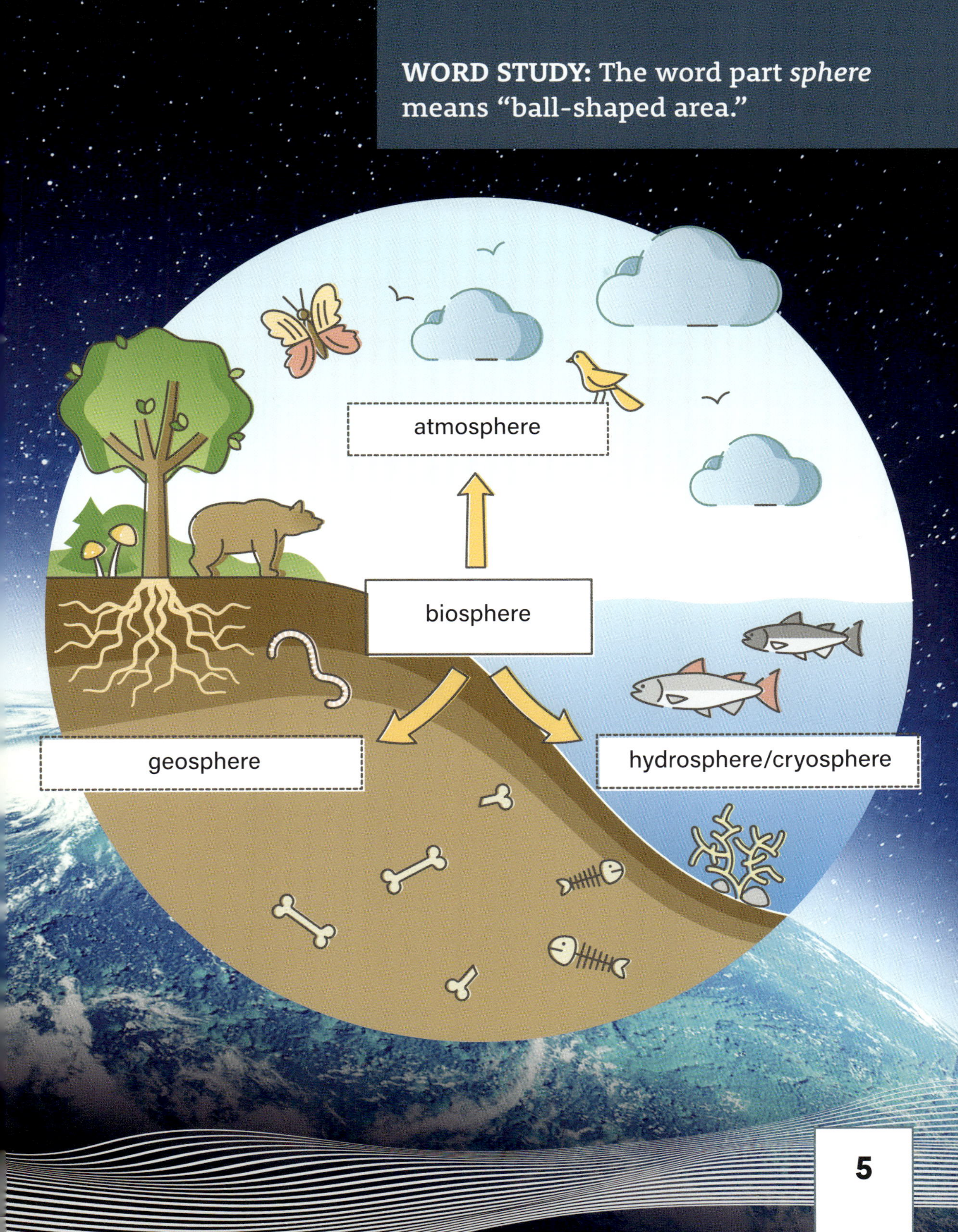

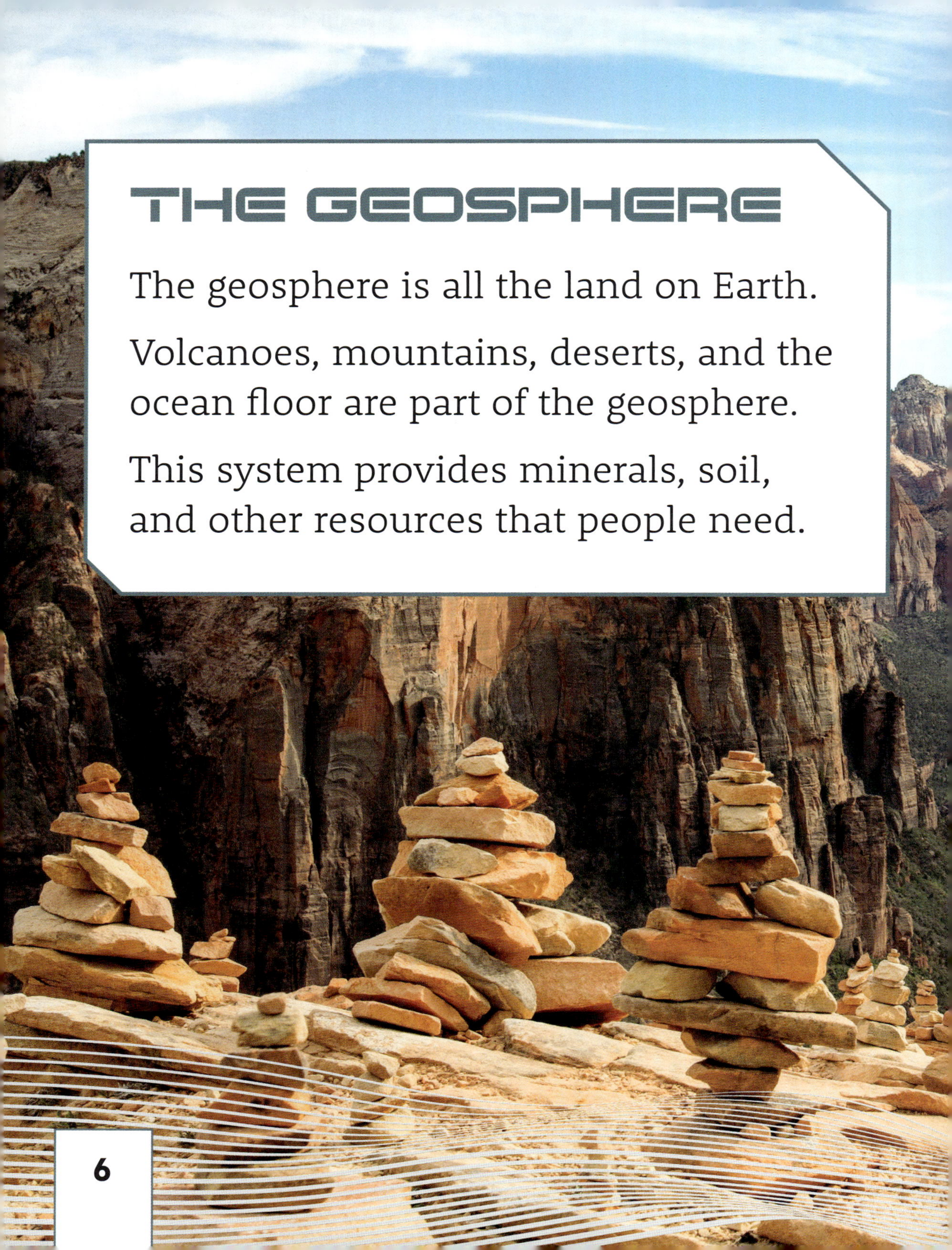

THE GEOSPHERE

The geosphere is all the land on Earth.

Volcanoes, mountains, deserts, and the ocean floor are part of the geosphere.

This system provides minerals, soil, and other resources that people need.

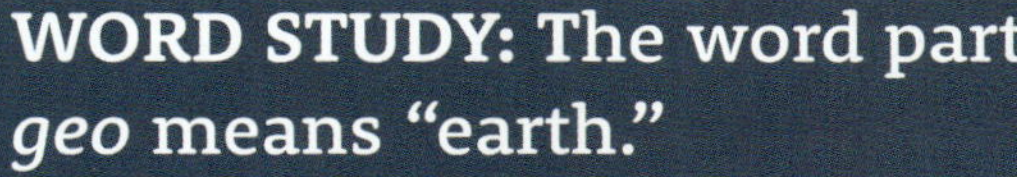

WORD STUDY: The word part *geo* means "earth."

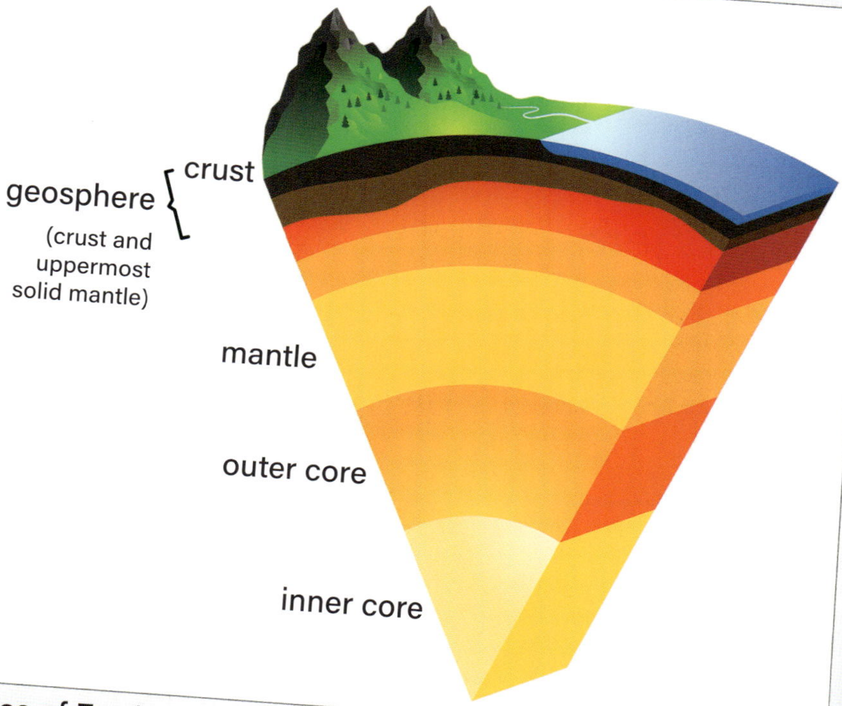

A slice of Earth shows the planet's layers.

THE HYDROSPHERE

The hydrosphere is all the water on Earth.

Oceans, rivers, **groundwater**, and melting **glaciers** are part of the hydrosphere.

This system provides the water that living things need to survive.

FUN FACTS

Oceans contain 97 percent of the water on Earth.

WORD STUDY: The word part *hydro* means "water."

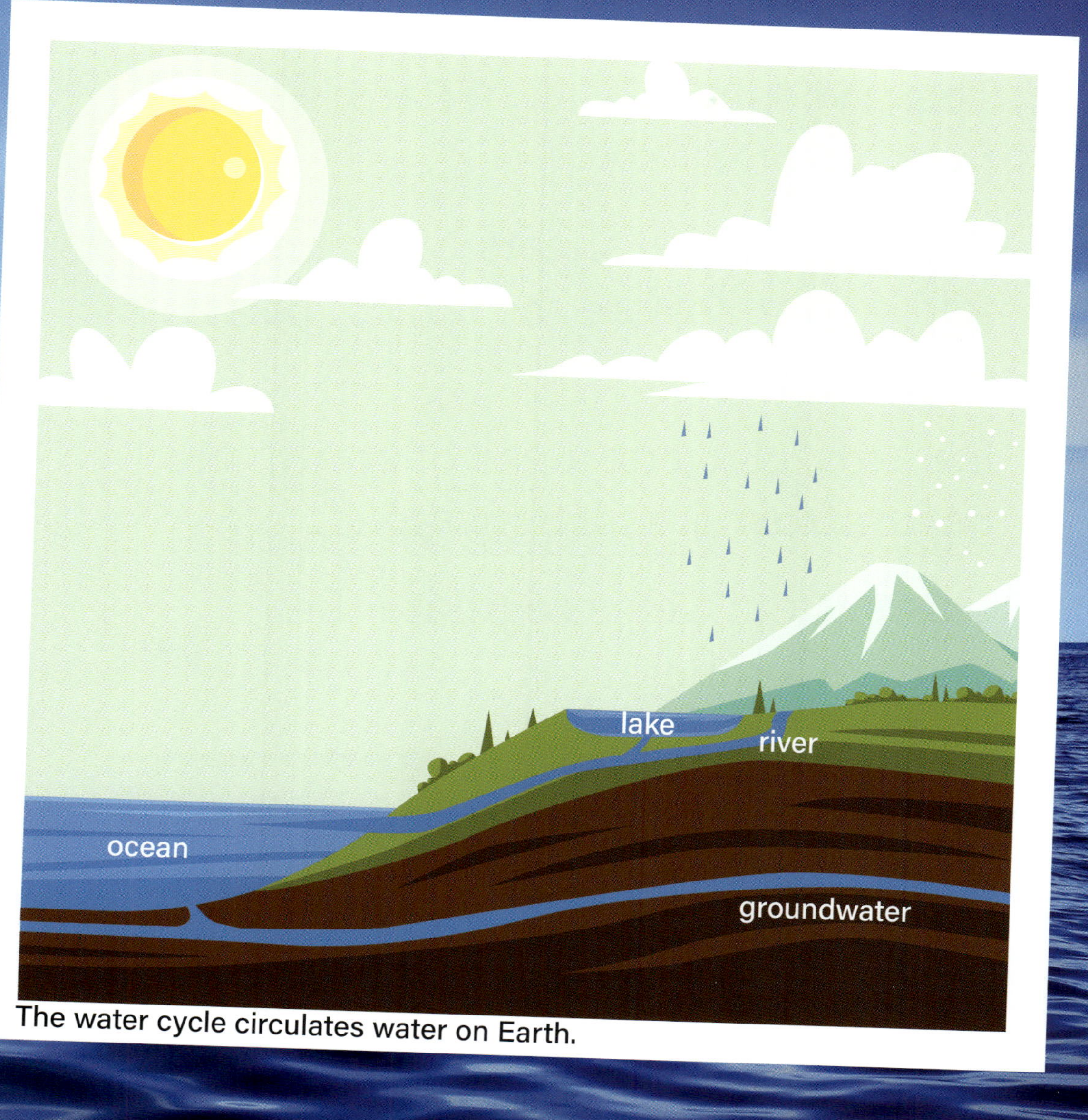

The water cycle circulates water on Earth.

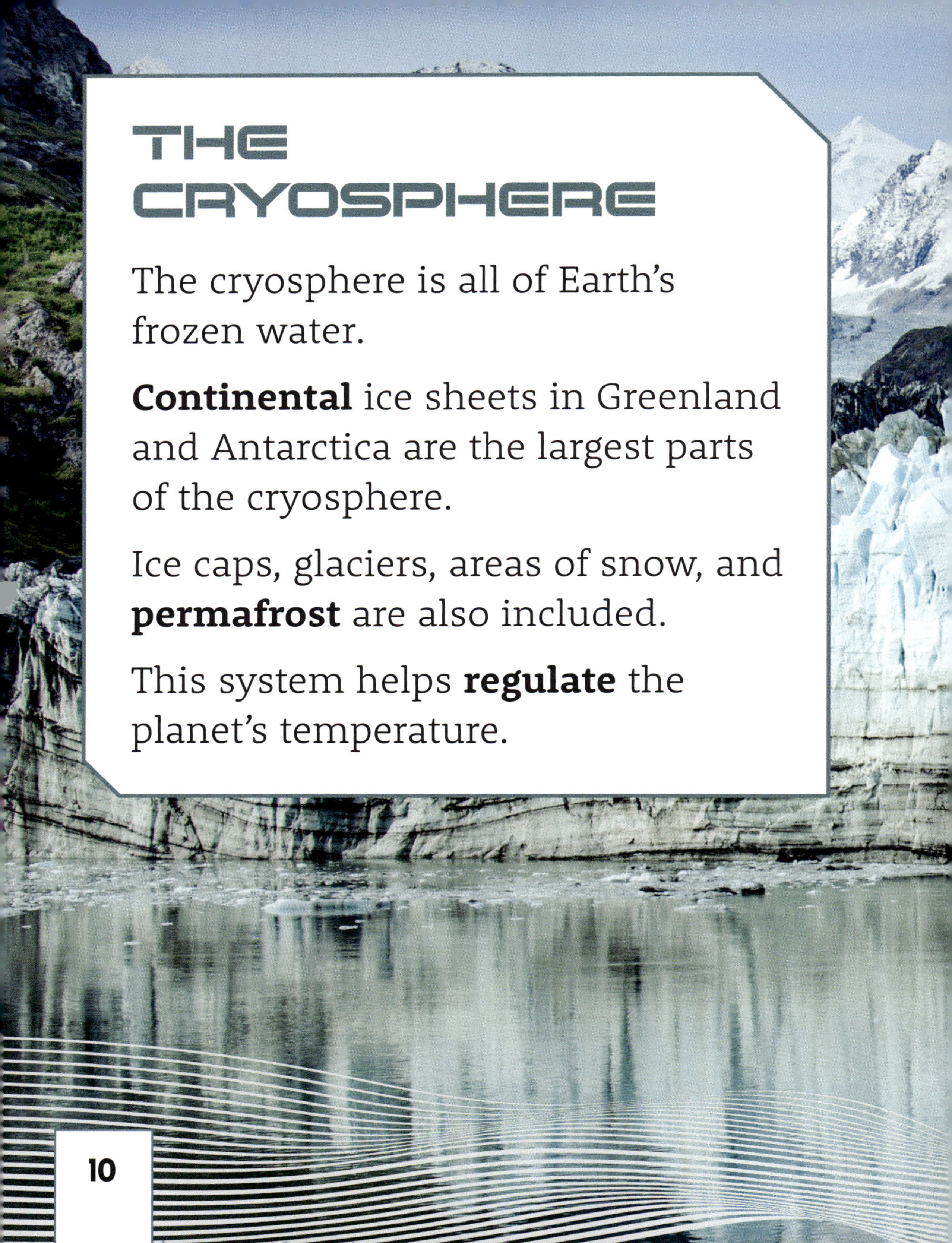

THE CRYOSPHERE

The cryosphere is all of Earth's frozen water.

Continental ice sheets in Greenland and Antarctica are the largest parts of the cryosphere.

Ice caps, glaciers, areas of snow, and **permafrost** are also included.

This system helps **regulate** the planet's temperature.

There are many forms of ice on Earth.

WORD STUDY: The word part *cryo* means "cold."

THE ATMOSPHERE

The atmosphere is all the gases that surround Earth.

It is made up of five layers between the planet's surface and space.

Earth is the only planet we know that has the gases needed to support life.

This system is responsible for Earth's weather.

FUN FACTS

Earth's atmosphere is 78 percent nitrogen and 21 percent oxygen.

WORD STUDY: The word part *atmo* means "air."

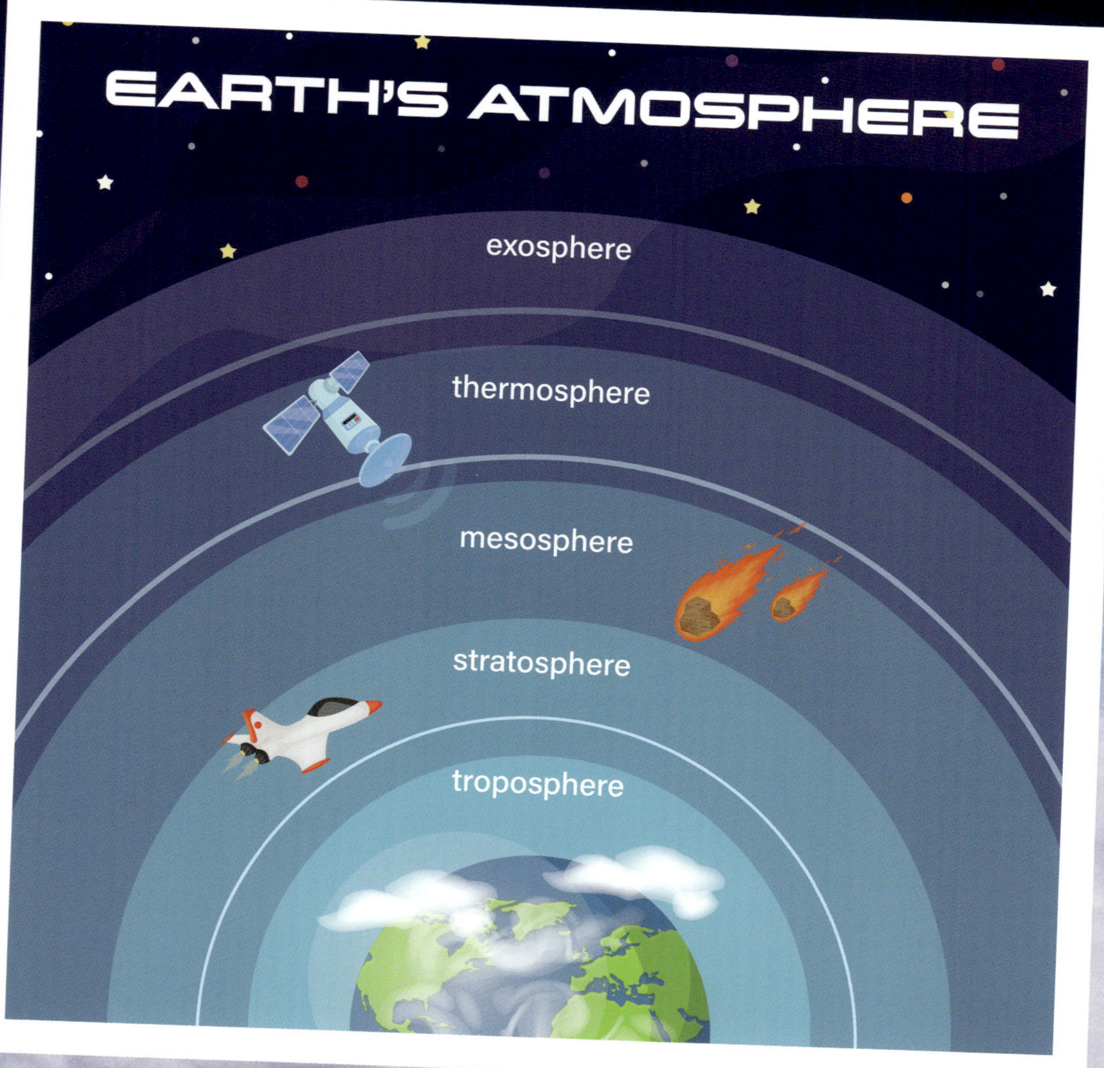

THE BIOSPHERE

The biosphere is all living things on Earth.

It is organized into **ecosystems** that living things depend on to survive.

Humans, animals, plants, and bacteria are part of the biosphere.

FUN FACTS

There may be as many as 30 million species of plants and animals on Earth. Most have not been identified.

WORD STUDY: The word part *bio* means "life."

Living things need each other to survive.

EARTH MATERIALS

Earth materials are four important resources found in Earth's crust.

They are the building blocks of Earth's systems. They sustain life.

1. Minerals are solid substances that occur naturally and that do not come from plants or animals.
2. Rocks are solids made of minerals and mineral-like substances.
3. Soil is **decayed** plants and animals mixed with broken bits of rocks.
4. Water is necessary for all living things.

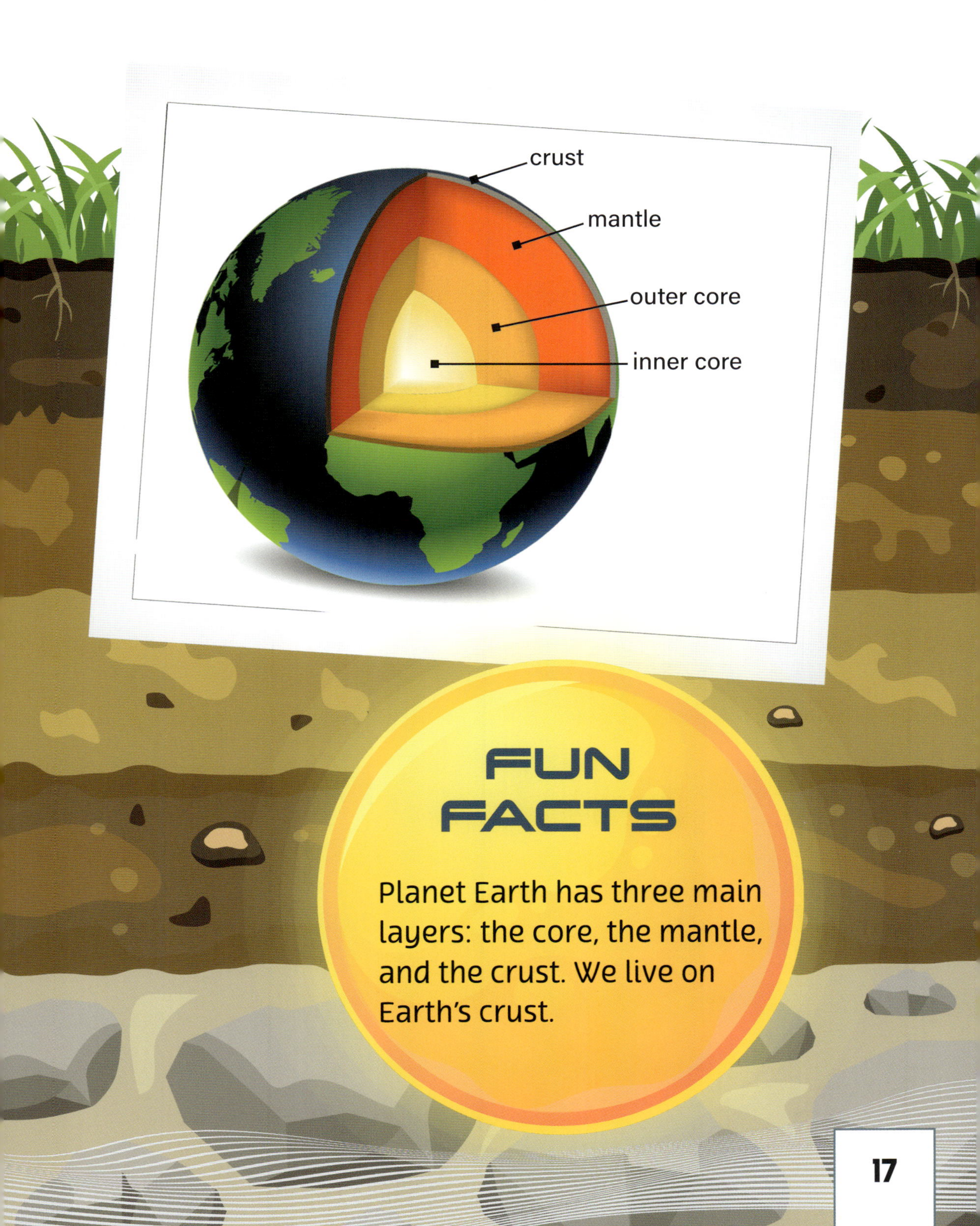

FUN FACTS

Planet Earth has three main layers: the core, the mantle, and the crust. We live on Earth's crust.

CAREER: GLACIOLOGIST

Glaciologists study how ice makes changes to Earth.

They research the effects of climate change on glaciers and ice caps.

They also collect data about ice discovered on moons and other planets.

INVESTIGATE: RISING SEA LEVELS

Materials:

- Two plastic storage containers about six inches (15 centimeters) square
- Permanent marker
- Clay or Play-Doh
- 12 to 20 ice cubes
- Water
- Ruler

Procedure:

(1) Use the marker to label one container *Glacier* and the other *Iceberg*.

(2) Press equal amounts of clay into one end of each container to represent land. Make the land flat and smooth. The remainder of each container will represent the ocean.

(3) In the *Glacier* container, place as many ice cubes as possible on the land.

(4) In the *Iceberg* container, put the same number of ice cubes in the ocean.

(5) Pour water into the *Iceberg* container just until the ice floats. Make sure the level of the water is lower than the land.

(6) Pour the same amount of water into the ocean in the *Glacier* container. Do not pour water over the land or the ice cubes.

(7) Use the marker to carefully draw a line on the outside of each container to show the water level. Use the ruler to measure the water level and record.

(8) Allow the water in both containers to melt completely.

(9) Check the water level lines on both containers.

(10) Measure the water levels with the ruler. Did the level rise in one or both containers? How do your findings relate to global sea-level rise?

THE SCIENTIFIC METHOD

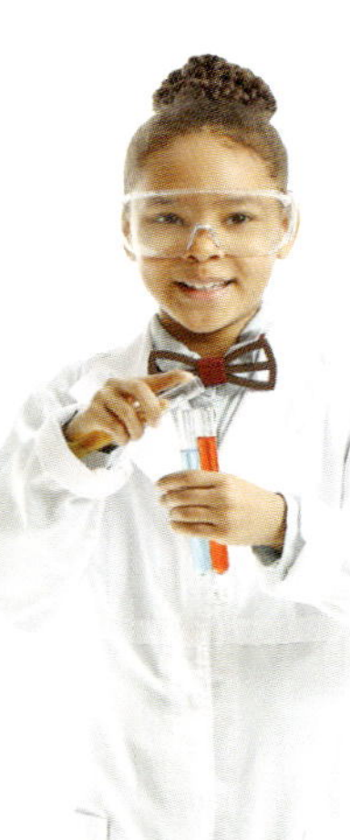

- Ask a question.
- Gather information and observe.
- Make a hypothesis or guess the answer.
- Experiment and test your hypothesis, or guess.
- Analyze your test results.
- Modify your hypothesis, if necessary.
- Make a conclusion.

SCIENTIST SPOTLIGHT

Christopher Jackson is a geologist and an adventurer. He has worked for companies and universities. His research focuses on how changes on Earth affect the way soil collects and settles. During his work on *Expedition Volcano*, a TV documentary, he spent a week camping next to a lake of lava. Jackson encourages scientists to use their knowledge and skills to help the planet.

GLOSSARY

continental (KAHN-tuh-nen-tuhl): forming or belonging to a continent, a large continuous mass of land

decayed (di-KAYD): rotted and broken down

ecosystems (EE-koh-sis-tuhmz): groups of living things that share an environment and that depend on each other

glaciers (GLAY-shurz): slow-moving rivers of ice

groundwater (GROUND-waw-tur): water held underground in soil or in the pores of rocks

interacts (in-tur-AKTS): reacts to one another; becomes involved with or affects others

permafrost (PUR-muh-frawst): permanently frozen soil in cold areas of Earth

regulate (REG-yuh-late): to control, manage, or adjust

resources (REE-sor-sis): things that are of value or use, especially those that come from the Earth

systems (SIS-tuhmz): groups of related things that work together as an interconnecting network

INDEX

AFTER READING QUESTIONS

1. Name Earth's five major systems.
2. Describe ways that one system could impact another.
3. Why are Earth's materials important?

ABOUT THE AUTHOR

Christina Earley lives in South Florida with her husband, son, and dog. Her favorite subject in school was science. She enjoys learning the science behind the world around her, such as how roller coasters work. She loves mint chocolate chip ice cream and mermaids.

Written by: Christina Earley
Design by: Kathy Walsh
Editor: Kim Thompson

Photographs/Shutterstock: Cover & Title pg, p 2, 3: Photobank.kiev.ua, Aksenova Nadezhd, amudsenh; p 4-23: amudsenh; p 4, 8, 12, 14, 17: Hlidskjalf; p 4: ixpert; p 5: VectorMine; p 7: evenfh, VectorMine; p 8: Songchai W; p 9: Platon Anton; p 10: lembi; p 11: VectorMine; p 12: leeborn; p 13: CRStocker; p 14: Simileus; p 15: VectorMine; p 16: Yuliya_vector; p 17: Webspark; p 18: luchschenF; p 19: polarman; p 21: @Wiki, Pixel-Shot

Library of Congress PCN Data
Earth Systems / Christina Earley
Earth and Space Science
ISBN 979-8-8873-5358-6 (hard cover)
ISBN 979-8-8873-5443-9 (paperback)
ISBN 979-8-8873-5528-3 (EPUB)
ISBN 979-8-8873-5613-6 (eBook)
Library of Congress Control Number: 2022951338

Printed in the United States of America.

Seahorse Publishing Company
www.seahorsepub.com

Published in the United States
Seahorse Publishing
PO Box 771325
Coral Springs, FL 33077